The BROKEN
STRING

Books by Grace Schulman

Poetry

The Broken String
Days of Wonder: New and Selected Poems
The Paintings of Our Lives
For That Day Only
Hemispheres
Burn Down the Icons

Translation

At the Stone of Losses: Poems by T. Carmi
Songs of Cifar (with Ann McCarthy de Zavala)
 by Pablo Antonio Cuadra

Criticism

Marianne Moore: The Poetry of Engagement

Editions

The Poems of Marianne Moore
Ezra Pound

The
BROKEN
STRING

GRACE SCHULMAN

Houghton Mifflin Company

BOSTON   NEW YORK   2007

For information about permission to reproduce selections from
this book, write to Permissions, Houghton Mifflin Company,
215 Park Avenue South, New York, New York 10003.

Visit our Web site: www.houghtonmifflinbooks.com.

Library of Congress Cataloging-in-Publication Data
Schulman, Grace.
   The broken string / Grace Schulman.
      p. cm.
   Includes bibliographical references.
   ISBN-13: 978-0-618-44370-3
   ISBN-10: 0-618-44370-3
   1. Music — Poetry.   2. New York (N.Y.) — Poetry.
      3. Long Island (N.Y.) — Poetry.   I. Title.
   PS3569.C538B76 2007
   811'.54 — dc22   2006026928

Printed in the United States of America

MP 10 9 8 7 6 5 4 3 2 1

My thanks to the editors of the following journals in which these poems appeared, often
in earlier versions: *American Scholar*: "Headstones." *Atlantic Monthly*: "Cimicifuga." *Barrow Street*: "Late Snow." *Cimarron Review*: "Chosen," "Harp Song," "Loss," "Lesson from
the Coin," "Rain Downtown," "Waves." *DoubleTake*: "In the Foreground." *Georgia Review*: "Art Tatum at the Gee-Haw Stables," "The Broken String," "First Nights." *Kenyon
Review*: "The Letter B," "The Fifth of July." *Michigan Quarterly Review*: "Kol Nidrei,
September 2001." *Paris Review*: "The Footbridge." *Pleiades*: "Joy." *Prairie Schooner*: "Origins," "Orson's Shadow," "Speak, Memory." *Rattapallax*: "Blue in Green." *Sewanee Review*: "Apples" (as "Apples on Lower Fifth Avenue"), "From the New World," "Query,"
"Readers," "Thelonious Himself." *Western Humanities Review*: "The Crow Man," "Death,"
"The Horror," "The Row."

   "Headstones" received the *American Scholar* Award for Best Poem of 2004. "First
Nights" was reprinted in *Never Before: Poems about First Experiences*, edited by Laure-Anne Bosselaar. "In the Foreground" reappeared in *110 Stories*, edited by Ulrich Baer. "Kol
Nidrei, September 2001" was heard on www.fathom.com. "Apples" was reprinted in the
Poetry Calendar 2007, edited by Shafiq Naz.

   I'm grateful to the John Simon Guggenheim Foundation for endowing this collection.
My thanks to Baruch College, CUNY, for their continuing faith, and to the MacDowell
Colony, for freedom to pursue the work.

For Jerome L. Schulman

The roll, the rise, the carol, the creation.

— Gerard Manley Hopkins

CONTENTS

1

2

3

4

5

1

THE BROKEN STRING

I

When Itzhak Perlman raised his violin
and felt the string snap, he sank and looked down
at legs unfit to stand and cross the stage
for a replacement. He bowed to the maestro,
played radiant chords, and finished the concerto

with the strings he had. Rage forced low notes
as this surf crashes on rock, turns, and lifts.
Later, he smiled and said it's what you do:
not just play the score, but make new music
with what you have, then with what you have left.

2

What you have left: Bill Evans at the keyboard,
Porgy. The sound rose, but one note, *unworthy,*
stalled in his head above the weightless chords,
above the bass, the trumpet's holler: *Porgy.*
A sudden clenched fist rose, pounded the keys,

fell limp: a heroin shot had hit a nerve.
I Loves You, Porgy. Sundays at the Vanguard
he soloed, improvised — his test that starved
nameless fear. Hands pitted against each other,
like the sea's crosscurrents, played away anger.

3

My father bowed before the Knabe piano,
scanned notes, touched fingers lightly, and began,
by some black art, I thought, his hearing gone
for years. And always, Mozart, Liszt, Beethoven.
One day I gasped, for there were runs

he never heard, played as a broken kite string
launches a lifelike eagle that might soar
on what the flier holds, what he has left.
Not even winds that howl along these shores
and raise the surf can ever ground that flight.

THE LETTER B

In the beginning was the letter B.
Through B, God made the world. Today that sign

gleams on a keyboard for neither cadenzas
nor waterfall arpeggios, but for prayers

tapped out on keys that flicker like strung beads,
paper-thin, like pearly yellow seashells

tide washes in. I count on weightier strokes
by surer hands with trowels that dug out sound,

B at the base. For the B that blooms now,
curved like a bellflower in high wind,

a Phoenician sailed the letter *beth*
to the Greeks for *beta,* centuries ago.

B is for B.C.E., for Nestor's cup,
for the stone scratches on a burial urn,

and for Babel's blankness when our languages
were undone; B is for bare winters

of the untaught, for slaves' songs bellowed out
on a free night, and for the blessed who learned

to write them down. B is for Hector's burial,
and for the bending of angry Achilles

who, when he remembers his own dead father
he will not see again, gives up the body,

and the Trojans buried Hector, breaker of horses.
B is for barbed rage, and for the bond

between one and another, and how the two
enfold, like buxom curves of the letter B,

and how, braided together, they brew words
benign and bellicose, brash and believing,

bits of ourselves strewn, rooted, over time.
B, the blaze of black fire on white fire,

the Torah's letters, blares at the center,
bottom row, where my lines are born.

The Fifth of July

Hot sun again. Coda to last night's flares
that rose in giant O's and fell in tears,
a lowdown blue-note soprano sax blares
"O beautiful," razz for the morning after.
Flags snap in pride, but pride flags in the fire
of headline deaths, and high convictions lie
like fizzled-out red crackers on the shore,
now litter for the pick-up volunteers.
Up headland, the tide licks ochre stones
as though to coax their spirit, one by one,
in shallows, to lift up in the clean vapor

still found in road-sign names of English settlers —
and in a photo of Moses, my great-uncle,
who grins at me now, strutting army medals
of World War I. He was prized as the first
born here to foreign parents on a past
Fourth of July. O season of sky flashes,
give me instead dim lights of fireflies,
milky lampshells, stars, and bayberry candles
of uncertainty, the rosebush on sand
burning but uncharred. Limits. An old shepherd
ambling across the shore and sniffing driftwood.

QUERY

Is there a healing twig or plume,
a rod or wizard's tea, a spell,
a paste of flowers and their stems
to lift my love and make him whole?

I'd see him take these rocky stairs
two after two, down to a park
that overflows with sycamores
whose twisted limbs have just come back

to sprout, renewed, on paths so thin,
so dense with green, he'd lose his way,
search for an iron bridge or pond,
and know, just as a ball let fly

sails back, he would walk out again.
When science shrugs, where is the stone
that mends, the dung beetle that cures.
Or, surely if some words on fire

can kill, others can right a wrong.
Shaman, teach me a chant to ban
pain. For it, take all my songs,
whose cures, if any, are unknown.

HEADSTONES

Twin tidelines of shells gleam on wet sand
like a giant's tire tracks: fluted white chips,
cracked blues, a purple comma, shards of whelks
the Montauks whittled down to beads and strung

as wampum, shining barter for protection
against attack. What strategy, that art.
I see the Montauk sachem Wyandanch,
offered knives for land, crave only muxes —

drills for threading clamshells into necklaces.
Sell these plains, why not — only in name,
after all — besides, he would have given
land and sea, with all its whales, for peace.

Yes, he would sign their scrawled-on page, his stamp
no X but two stick figures, their hands clasped.
Hands fell as leaves. Wyandanch dead,
his language failed, names faded that had vowels

like gulls' cries: *Poniut, Sassakato,*
never on headstones. In a nameless grave,
diggers found clamshell money strung with weeds,
struck with the island's sand-and-water face,

strewn like coins in Egypt's tombs, new mintings
whose glossy hollows stored a people's prayers
and tagged the one who wore them: powerful,
now holier for being buried fire.

The town yacht club has "headstones" — gazing photos,
racing trophies. Once, as a dinner guest,
I drove past roads with names of English counties,
Norfolk and Kent, then found a seaside table.

Wyandanch would not have been invited,
nor would my grandfather Dave, much less
my ancestor Schmuel, but there I was,
staring at shell toss, hearing breakers roar:

Wyandanch and *Quashashem*, his daughter,
her name the sound of seawater through stones,
snapped shells their monument, their living marker.
Sun gone, white jackets circled linen,

the voices swelled, long open vowels rolled in,
sharp consonants clicked and crackled with the surf
to drown out even the historical
cannon fire when men lowered the flag.

Blue in Green

Blue in green: baywater seen through grasses
that quiver over it, stirring the air,
slanted against the water's one-em dashes.
Each blade is a brushstroke on thin rice paper,

unrehearsed, undrafted, no revision,
right on the first take. In "Blue in Green,"
on tenor sax, John Coltrane fills the blues
with mournful chords on scales older than Jubal's,

ending in air. He'd not played it before
that recording, with that piano and bass
rising alone and, birds in flight, together.
Right on the first take. Improvisation,

he called it, but it must have been foreseen,
like the painter's brushstroke. A wrong line
could blot the composition, snag the paper.
It had to be unstudied, like a tern's cry,

and natural, like a rope's clink on a mast
with wind as bass player, huge and invisible.
If only I could remember the past
without regret for the windrose petal's fall,

for words unspoken, and without remorse
for loves withheld. Rough-draft mistakes.
If only my heart could teach my hands
to play, and get it right on the first take.

THE FOOTBRIDGE

Facing wisteria that turned soot-gray,
Monet painted a footbridge over a pond,
dawn, noon, sundown. Seeing neither violet

nor red, only ice blue, he gazed at willows
no longer willows, and cried for the sun
that would always outblaze new city lights.

Just as his eyesight failed, his vision grew.
In *Japanese Bridge,* green loops span two banks
as they might touch two continents. Two centuries.

Wild hair entangles someone else's dreams —
the painter's hand moved to a watery plant,
deep-set, that surfaced and broke into flame.

Here at Parson's Pond, I keep that flame.
I'd planned to cross the footbridge that goes nowhere,
with planks that snake from woods into more woods

and end in gloom. I took a safer route
instead, and saw the arch mirrored in water
where wind stirred bony legs that fell in place

intact, as though it sank and rose again.
November. No sleet as yet, no chill.
Even swamp oaks held leaves. Wind warped the pond's

mirror-footbridge into an abstraction
in fire colors, come up from silt to try me
on this clear day in my figural world.

Kol Nidrei, September 2001

All vows are canceled now,
all words undone like chains
that snap, their lockets smashed.
All sentences cut short,

main clauses powerless
to govern their dependents
or lead the voice in prayer.
All syllables annulled.

Verbs lag. All images
envisioned by blind eyes.
All penciled lines erased
that trembling hands composed.

My court, a grove at sundown:
sun rays pour through stiff branches,
unearthly yet of earth;
stump of a fallen oak

whose mate once flourished green
and now looms red and yellow
like towers burst into flame.
No ark with scrolls, no benches,

no prayer shawls, holy books,
or ram's horn. Only trees
stand witness in this silence,
and autumn's humid air

blurs a bark's crevices.
As this cloud turns to vapor,
all forms circle in smoke,
all promises unravel,

all pages torn to shreds
and blown to drift in wind
whose words cannot reveal
the truth of what I've seen.

2

First Nights

The best of all was listening to a hush
under the chandelier that never fell
and the fat box adorned with gilded masks.

When stiff asbestos parted over velvet,
my father gasped. He'd left the stage for a desk
when I was born. And now first nights were holy.

A program and a house called the Majestic,
more than prayer book and shul, called forth his praise.
One night an actor, fake wrinkles, white hair,

cried out under his breath, *All-shaking thunder*,
hoarse as my father, who had scared me once,
shutting a book and crying to some storm,

Arms, arms, sword, fire. That night, pitched forward,
I clutched a lineny square, but no tears came
for that desperate king until the swords

I suddenly thought real clashed for his throne.
Exits, applause, and I could breathe again.
My father said, "It helps us bear God's silences,"

and I knew watching was a kind of prayer,
a make-believe you play by looking hard.
It lifted him, as when, evenings at home,

dead still in thoughts about his sister lost,
he heard of cities bombed, while there, onstage,
Lear shouted, in a whisper, *Mad, sweet heaven.*

ORSON'S SHADOW

Wall-to-wall murals of *Les Tuileries*.
Smell of starched linen and midget white lilies.
My father asks, over steaming quenelles
again, why quit a writing job to write?

The magazine, where my boss wears spike heels,
curses in French, commands in bold italics,
and hints at early breakfasts with the Windsors,
wants nouns that float. I'd have verbs feet-to-fire.

Dad tries to understand. I understand
only now that his Beaune at La Caravelle
consoles for hunger as a child in Poland.
There, facing us, from a wide round of tables

is the wide, round, fat face of Orson Welles,
smiling at us — no, at his chanterelles.
I smile back at his magic: *Touch of Evil*.
Citizen Kane. The Martians. The Martians.

Nothing lately, except, over cartoons,
the voice that soars, that peals like deep-tone bells.
Fade out the fat-cheek face of Orson Welles.
Fade in my father, who, despite my perils,

blooms, an elm replanted in new soil.
Two men. The past — one's rise, the other's fall —
is over now. I can't weep, not at all,
nor, like the others, savor crème caramel

for my own past, which has not yet begun.
I press a lily into the first press run
of my first book, slide it onto his table,
join Dad, and flee — to keep that present tense.

Thelonious Himself

They came back new each night: thumps, craggy runs,
one-finger jabs at keys that were hot pans.
Heels dug in wood, soles flapping like seals,
he stabbed notes that seemed wrong until they soared,

all ragged beauty. Just twenty-five, I envied
his starry reach, the risk to play it real.
At the slick magazine, the risk was only
no risk. I stabbed a lukewarm keyboard,

hard prose about airy tulle. Form meant neat,
no dissonance. Once I was tapped to herd
Ten Best-Dressed College Girls to hear the Monk
in a café on St. Marks Place. Not bad.

Now *there* was neatness. Strict as shorebirds grouping
they filed in, breadknife heels clacking in tempo;
strangled waists, sleek heads acclaiming finish.
Ten S-shapes, twenty legs Monk ogled through

dark glasses, bamboo frames. He didn't sneer
at their clatter. No, while the sax wailed, solo,
Monk stood tall and swayed forward, unmistakably
davening, moved by some unseen beauty.

Suddenly he snapped fingers as though
to shape pain into order. That was form.
And all was void, as before Creation,
and there was light. I left the job next day.

Origins

After boisterous storms, by God's providence,
we espied land. We anchored in the bay,
compassed about to the very sea with oaks,
pines, juniper, sassafras, a harbor,
wherein a thousand sail of ships may safely ride.

That *Mayflower* Pilgrim wrote nothing of winds,
the cracked mast, hunger, deaths, two months at sea.
Instead, he fixed on landing, when stark wonder
forced up words that named each thing he saw:
oaks, pines, juniper, sassafras, a harbor.

·

When my grandfather's ship steamed in from Belgium
to Castle Garden, once an opera house,
he thought he heard dense seawalls ring with arias.
He searched for hope. No tales of filth, the dead,
unbroken skies. Instead, hands cradling tea,

he spun stories of how he'd combed the decks
for new talk wafting past him. His parents frowned,
torn, for they had sailed to find free schools,
but held fast to the old talk, handed down,
unwritten. If that were lost, their origins

would drown under black waves. I found his journal
in spidery gothic script, of English words
denoting change, rain *freezes, glistens, shines,*
and contraries, the small lot on the corner,
words like his socks, unmatched but worn together.

Years later, he read law that promised fixity,
rules to keep order. Even as he walked
through courthouse columns, soldierly in granite,
he jotted words about words, *motley, impure.*
They rise out of the sea, a congregation

of forebears, thieves, or blameless villagers.
I never knew them. That regret itself
prints vivid images of Bens and Esthers,
Daves and Roses bent to offer blessings,
of others on shipboard intoning *aves,*

hosannas, and *Lord, Lord*'s, not murmured,
as in a church, but shouted up to God,
as though their very singing would turn fear
to hope, *wanhope,* the root of both.
At night I hear them roar against high waves:

ghosts, from *hostis,* root of friend and stranger,
immigrants collecting words with dread,
as ships grow barnacles that slow their hulls,
and with joy, as sea rocks in nuns' habits
burst into color, sprouting red mosaic,

green wrack, and yellow poppies. Drifting in,
immigrants, broken, snapped off from their past
and made whole again like the nouns they hoard
that signal change and garner opposites
in a fierce current that flows through me.

Collectors

I

Pablo Neruda scrawled his odes on a table
made from a plank he saw the tide wash in.
It came to hold his lilies, bread, and salt.

He dusted things he'd found — hammer, scythe, lantern,
anchor at rest, too rusty for new sailing —
and stroked invisible handprints for the wear

of farmers, carpenters, sculptors of lambs.
When soldiers sacked his home in Valparaiso,
they smashed the table and shattered a horse

of painted wood that lay done for, legs split,
bit in the open mouth, snuffling the dust,
and clubbed a figurehead the sea bleached white.

She fell, head thrown back, grand, as on her prow,
blind eyes staring at some sea god in sorrow.
Only cracked lamps shone, brighter — in his art.

2

Noah and sons, ancestral collectors,
rescued beasts from the flood. Hie, you pairs
of auks, shamirs! Come ziz, ruler of birds,

eels, and salamanders! He set them free
and they lived on. Here, a stone jar gapes empty
and a tray rests that held tears of a woman

who washed her brass with sand on a far shore.
They tell me who I am: the last heir of immigrants
whose silver, never polished to preserve shadows,

and potbellied jugs that had belonged to others
were amulets, like pitchers in Dutch paintings
made to assure the burgher's immortality.

The sea-blue goblets I gave to friends
are never owned. They ring for those who raise them.
Raise them now and reach for many hands.

3

Finders, not keepers. Guardians, sometimes fixers
of the one-legged chair, the wingless bird,
the wounded giltwood table. Once my mother

glued on the toppled head of an ivory Buddha
and placed it near patched-up St. Jude, a likeness
of the apostle, specialist in crisis

during my father's sickness. Dad complained
that nicked statues dismayed, whether devotional
or art, and searching eyes set him on edge —

but he recovered. Gods live in things
rescued, painted, scrubbed, and passed on. Collectors,
save things that will save us. Pack them now

for when the sky clears, clocks and ladles, angels
caught in flight, a sewing machine, spades
for the new plantings, justice, laughter, poems.

Art Tatum at the Gee-Haw Stables

Hands flew across the keys like osprey wings
in high wind. Solo flight. He played alone

and cursed blurred sight, quicksilver notes unblurred.
Uptown, after hours, he cast out

the tell-it-all-to-God, blessed-be-His-name,
whatever-else-might-come fury and grief.

Uptown was where the real arpeggios soared,
in "Sweet Lorraine" and "Georgia on My Mind,"

where eyelids covered visions like an ark
as he trilled a hymn he'd picked out once

when keys danced to his father's harp, to strings
of a steel-pipe mechanic, after hours.

Here the boss tapped a whisk broom on newspaper,
and the frail stride piano outshone the grand

earlier, on Fifty-second Street,
where white faces had gasped, stunned by the speed

and accuracy of two-handed runs,
never to know that when he left there, caneless,

and taxied uptown, he, the put-on artist,
sang out after hours, and for God.

JOY

The crowd yells, stamping, for the "Ode to Joy"
that swells to close Beethoven's Ninth Symphony,
played when the night air thickens with cries —
deaths by gunfire and a trespassing sea.

They always shout for it, the tease of hope,
the lure of gladness. I've heard that when
the deaf composer led the first performance,
he flailed both arms after the music stopped

until an alto turned him clear around
to see them screaming. He bowed, not in joy
but prayer, the doubt more real than the possession.
Beethoven set the ode to notes so high
and so low that no chorus can sing joy
without a struggle — and that's the point.

      ·

Turner, who saw mud rivers shine in fog,
hunched in a cellar and one day a week
flung open pine shutters and cried: "What jewels!"
As a boy, he curled up in a brig's bow

to see skies whiter over murky waters.
I think of him this zero January
of prose chatter, nightfall at four-thirty.
Sometimes diamonds glitter in dark snow

layered with filth, and track you down dirt streets
the way a Byzantine Madonna's halo
some monk made into gold from egg tempera
can follow shining after you've walked on.
Emerson's *wild delight*. All I cannot fathom.
All that I imagine, therefore am.

.

Joy's ode: the unexpected transformation,
the flight, the mystery of what is given,
tentative, unasked for, and uncertain
yet sure, the words I never knew were there.

3

The Horror

Soutine created light
at the heart of dread
by dragging a steer's carcass
up to his rooms in Paris.

It twisted on a rack
like a tormented saint
while he watched from his easel,
casement windows shut

to shelter canvases.
When flies crowded the flesh
and hid its pinks and scarlets,
he paid a ragged model

to sit beside the corpse
and fan insects away.
Of course, it decomposed.
He hefted pails of blood

he'd carried from the market
and sloshed them over rot
to restore the gleam.
Sickened, weak from hunger

(he scarcely ate for days
to stoke a greedier fire),
Soutine attacked the canvas,
slashing with palette knife.

He slapped on reds for legs
and shoulders with a brush
that sprang in arabesques
and sucked as it pulled away

like seawater from rocks.
Fingers smeared the haunch
with white-yellow swervings
until an incandescence

leaped out of the carrion
like the sky's fire at dawn.
Garnets and rubies glowed
from the massive hulk.

He sliced air with his brush
that had transfigured it.
When neighbors reported odors
of decaying flesh,

Soutine harangued inspectors
about the health of art.
He never explained his task:
to look into death's hide

unflinching, to uncover
horror as it is,
and in a putrid room
turn flesh into light.

DEATH

Kaddish that sanctifies and praises being.
Black fire on moss: the grackle on the lawn
caught on fence wire, the nape still radiant,
yellow eye staring. The oak leaves I spread
that cover it. All but the yellow eye.

                    .

Loss that calls for exactitude, the urge
to render color: that bird's purple-black,
the green it fell on. The vivid thought
that changes shape and fades like a slow cloud,
scarlet azalea blossoms gone to straw.

                    .

In England's hills, a church marked by a skeleton
set over a bronze clock as though it might
gaze at daylight hours, if it had eyes;
in Mexico, on the Day of the Dead,
a girl in silk fondling her doll, a skull.

                    .

New Orleans: bystanders in undershirts,
in housedresses, follow a stranger's coffin
down to the church, to hum, croon, and ad-lib
"Call Jesus." Now the band picks up the hymn.
A sax keens low, subdued, tense with long waiting.

                    .

After the trumpet's dirge, after the burial,
jazzmen cut loose and blow the second-line beat,
up-tempo. Umbrellas open out like peonies
and spin with dancers. A snare drum seethes.
"Didn't He Ramble" raises up a life.

                    .

Spring rain that plays umbrellas like bass drums
soaks shoes of graveside kin who mumble Kaddish,
prayer with no word of death. Uncle Abe's sister
stands in the mire as though for penitence
and pivots from earth to fresh-cut grass.

.

The bowl she feeds him from, red-figured clay,
copied from one fired for a Spartan king
to sustain the journey. Her hand that flies
crazily off the page when she tries to sign
the DNR he ordered to let go.

.

The jewels warriors buried in Beowulf's barrow,
gold beakers and mead cups that thieves once dared
to drag from the hoard. Now let the earth have them
and cry to heaven the heirlooms are gone
that never were of use to the living.

.

Black woodsmoke that rose high over the barrow
roared to the sky and drowned their weeping
for their good lord's going. An old Geat woman
who sang grief, war, and slaughter would follow
Beowulf's time as the sky swallowed smoke.

.

The summer day when, poised to dive from rocks
into the sea, you reached out arms that still
wrap mine in sleep. The Etruscan king and queen
on a sarcophagus, under a shroud.
Under our paisley sheet. Years of our days.

St. Sulpice

Church bells. A racket of metallic rock.
A clown's babble over sidewalk speakers.

Inside brass doors, the odor of damp stone.
The tease of guttering candlelight on Jacob,

who lunges for the angel's chest. They struggle,
or are they dancing? Thighs entwine, hands clasp,

as in a glide-and-dip, feet stamp the ground
and kick high, frenzy held in check

as the two strut and grind, burning as one.
Jacob treads air, the angel's fleshy arms

flutter in human ectasy. A match
of love and rage, the wounding a fair price.

Once, in a house nearby, the painter Delacroix
envisioned the wrestlers in a knot of woods

and mixed russet browns for trees with branches
like witches' claws fanned out to raise the wind.

I see him wait, as I have, for an angel
to guide his hand, and not the one-night stand

who seems an angel until he leaves at dawn,
hides his own name but hurls another at you,

bitching and blessing. This Jacob's angel
is of earth, a man with imagined wings:

and there wrestled a man with him until daybreak.
Only the painting soars — by its maker's wings.

Outside the church, it's morning on the square.
A chestnut tree's pink blooms whiten in sun.

No din, just laughter from the street café.
My eyes smart in light. Nothing's the same.

The Crow Man

Ein jede Engel ist schrecklich.
Every angel terrifies.
— Rainer Maria Rilke

Snow whips the windshield full force, and in haze
a juniper stiffens in white surprise
like Dickinson's dress on a model in paradise.
Ermine mounds pile high and cover memories,

replacing houses, fields, and tawny geese.
Windshield wipers skid on crusted glass
and count lost seconds like a broken metronome.
I can't tell who, let alone where, I am.

My phone's unfit. Besides, I've lost my number,
my name, even my face in the rearview mirror.
And if I could connect, what words to offer:
Thaw the stew, love? No, silence is better.

FM news: *Car bomb kills seven soldiers* . . .
Static. A lost signal. Gray forms ahead
in fluff, in clarity. A roadside
crash. The driver who seems uninjured

shakes a fist, once at the other driver,
twice at the sky. *Danger, move to the edge,*
police broadcast, an impossible order.
Seven soldiers dead. Their faces merge

with those crash-dead, as far away or farther.
And then, corked in a bottle still afloat,
hoping to be more message than dead letter,
I see stillness. Exactitude. Measure.

Hidden in snow are trivialities
that have nothing to do with nothingness
where anything can happen — even, yes,
an angel. *Every angel terrifies,*

Rilke said, and I'll turn it around:
every terror that freezes words
and heightens glitter can summon an angel.
Besides, if an archangel once warbled

on a maple's highest bough in late sun,
a throne, at least, might tune up in this haze.
Seven soldiers dead, and here hot rage
mounts. FM again. A new voice utters:

*Find seven palaces with seven doors
to God's fiery robes.* No static interferes
with that starry command, the voice pure sapphire,
sparkling but husky, low, like a soft chord.

Dazzled, I fear that I might follow it,
with or without a highway exit sign.
A black shape flutters, wingless, into sight.
Is it a crow, for prey? I squint through panes

of ice. No, not a bird. A bulky man
lurches across what was a road to start
a stranger's car. At closer range,
I knew that I had seen him earlier

curse the storm and fight with other drivers
in a ballet of anger: thumbs, clenched fists,
lip-read insults. Now crows are everywhere.
Black parkas land, observe, and gather,

and vast boots track the stark clean lines of help.
When their hands and eyes emerge from the blur
on frosted glass, my face is in its mirror,
superimposed. Bellicose news will whirl

in zero winds again, but not here, now,
where no car swerves in snow
to pass another, in this calm center,
this white peace that calls for urgency.

Twilight now. With patience that is beauty,
the crow man, black-hooded hulk in mist,
flies from snow castles and rises from drifts,
healer of memory, bringer of life.

BORDERS

I

Perhaps because of the twiggy cigars
he offered me, the showy "Come, American,"
the outstretched hand, the hasty, sidelong stares
at shorts I packed to wear in white-hot sun,

at windblown hair, I knew he was a friend.
On my side of the gunfire, date-palm fronds
waved in groves. On his, white sand. In Kfar Saba,
they warned, don't walk the path too near the border.

Soldiers were shot, and would be, ours, theirs;
and new borders, none deadlier than the mind's.
Why was it then I had to cross, and why,
at that dizzying moment, fear disguised
as ignorance, I asked: "Where is the border?"
"Moved," he answered. "Now it is where you stand."

2

The numbers numb the deed. She was thirteen,
they noted, when they peered at sixteen feet
to "inspect the kill." She had crossed a line,
threadlike in white sun. The girl was shot.

I saw her name, Inam, today.
Its vowels roared over what numbers had told.
Thirteen. Twelve noon. A security area
ten yards wide. She skipped on that banned road,

some days her shortcut to a field of citrons
that seized her, or the red-and-white carnations
so plentiful they wither if ungathered,
or else in that bright air she could not fathom
those timeless warnings: *No, don't wander. Halt.
Don't look.* Or lose your love. Or turn to salt.

3

The lines I want are on the mezzo's pages
tonight, when she unlooses a Bach aria
to drift skyward: *Erbarme dich, have mercy,*
and when the chorus stands, sorrow and rage

in counterpoint, cross-rhythms, harmonies
and brawls, *Guard me* the cry of one alone
and everyone. All. For *St. Matthew Passion,*
read passion: the burn of grief, the rise of joy.

Four hundred daytimes snatched from the Leipzig choir,
and nights from children's squalls, went into notes,
one and one inked with wings, inside the bars,
or rows of threes and fours, freed by their limits
to swell beyond the church dome and strike fire,
blessed to transcend time, road lines, and borders.

4

FROM THE NEW WORLD

Orange alert has glared over this city
since terror acquired colors. Orange,
not yellow, not even yellow elevated.

Before Dvořák's Ninth, at Lincoln Center,
guards worry my handbag, stuffed with war news.
Oak leaves stick to pavement, yellow-to-orange

and high orange, brightest before they wither.
This year they sadden us. Talk was of endings,
not leaves but unrecurrent lives, and yet

with others now, we sink into a hush
like sanderlings that fly on a soundless cue.
Once the composer said his symphony

was Czech, as he was, that he added
"From the New World" in the final draft,
an offering for three years in America,

but in an oboe's long, plaintive vibrato,
I hear the phrases of Hasidic melodies,
African chants, come-thou's, and *kyries*

I caught once on a street corner downtown,
four blocks merging like a napkin's points.
I raced a traffic light's orange-to-red

to find a synagogue confronting churches,
Baptist and Roman, eyeing one another.
High above street whines, music soared in quarrels,

moans, blues, calls-and-responses, hymns that rose up
together from stone. It took a Czech patriot
to restore that day. Now the people cheer

so loud you'd think a New World is beginning,
the clamor telling us this world will do
as long as we can have some more of it.

Outside, the fountain shoots the stars.
We glance upward, smiling, even when
a leaf spins down to concrete, crisp, high orange.

Apples

Rain hazes a street cart's green umbrella
but not its apples, heaped in paper cartons,
dry under cling film. The apple man,

who shirrs his mouth as though eating tart fruit,
exhibits four like racehorses at auction:
Blacktwig, Holland, Crimson King, Salome.

I tried one and its cold grain jolted memory:
a hill where meager apples fell so bruised
that locals wondered why we scooped them up,

my friend and I, in matching navy blazers.
One bite and I heard her laughter toll,
free as school's out, her face flushed in late sun.

I asked the apple merchant for another,
jaunty as Cezanne's still-life reds and yellows,
having more life than stillness, telling us,

uncut, unpeeled, they are not for the feast
but for themselves, and building strength to fly
at any moment, leap from a skewed bowl,

whirl in the air, and roll off a tilted table.
Fruit-stand vendor, master of Northern Spies,
let a loose apple teach me how to spin

at random, burn in light and rave in shadows.
Bring me a Winesap like the one Eve tasted,
savored and shared, and asked for more.

No fool, she knew that beauty strikes just once,
hard, never in comfort. For that bitter fruit,
tasting of earth and song, I'd risk exile.

The air is bland here. I would forfeit mist
for hail, put on a robe of dandelions,
and run out, broken, to weep and curse — for joy.

Rain Downtown

Cold rain falls slant against a cupola,
drenches the greenmarket, mists windowpanes,
and in slow tempo wire-brushes umbrellas,
falling in buckets sent to mop us clean.

Rain lashes Hart Crane's house. Inside he utters,
Lo, Lord, Thou ridest, and raps his table
to drumbeats. Rain levels us all,
merchants and artists interchangeable,

bent by wet winds and twisted into Z's.
Rain clarifies. A woman bleared in haze
sees her image shine in a rainpool mirror,
lucid, undimmed, entwined with spindly trees.

From a high place where rivers overflow,
rain pummels a bus that will take us on
singly, in pairs. Rain soaks a newsprint photo
of a dead child. Perhaps it fogs my vision,

but I see rain blunt rage, and here are worthies:
a couple whose speech came in angry catcalls
as hands swiped air now bend over rubble
where someone slipped. Quiet. They help her rise.

Torrents wash tombstones in a tiny graveyard
crammed between rowhouses, and streams flush gutters.
Showers once nourished life before the flood
destroyed it. Rain, fall in peace on the square,

wipe away apathy and greed, come ranting,
surge, as after the sixth day of Creation,
when rain watered the land for the new plantings,
drizzle to downpour. And we were born.

Speak, Memory

No wrecking ball has ever smashed "our house,"
tall brick, a stone relief above the canopy
of monsters with pop eyes — to ward off danger.

The crosstown bus still snorts as it jerks east
to seas I'd read of at St. Agnes Library —
surely the patron saint of words — arched windows,

tables in stanzas. All's there, as it was.
Marigolds wilt in the same flower shop
and wilder greens crouch at the park's edge.

At home, the kid who clutches window bars
follows a hawk, archangel on an aerial;
three tower lights that, sleepless, I can watch

blink off at midnight. No lanes, only turrets
in view, I look up, never down at pavement
where rain, like tears, has washed off chalky scars.

On the street, a man berates his terrier
for yapping at a woman, paces behind,
who chides the man. No exit. The same brawl.

Safe home. Front door. But no, I am the stranger,
and cold. My key will never fit this lock.
Lost to a women's Gap is Blank's drugstore,

where girls in starched white middies swallowed malteds.
Gone, too, is Tarzan, stronger than warplanes.
The captain who left, khaki and small,

against the lobby's giant-chessboard floor.
The radio's drone. Uncle Josh, who played
a lute to drown the din. Father, who whispered "God"

in doubt, rattled his newspaper at towers
and stared, mute, at a photo of his sister,
a doctor who stayed in Warsaw with her patients.

His search. Bold scrawl in black ink on paper
crisp as dry leaves, a radiogram reply
in toneless caps: Helen lives. *Address unknown.*

(Facts came late: no escape, she climbed a tower,
tore down the Polish flag, leaped, and was shot.)
I lied. It was fear street. And it *has* changed,

all but for the gazing up at moons,
the wait for words like windows set in brick
that catch the light and open wide for hope.

THE ROW

A *Winter Wedding, Washington Square,*
oil on canvas, Fernand Lungren, 1897

Nothing is really lost. Take this white wedding,
for instance. After vows in the steeple church,
horse carriages file down to the Arch

along The Row, houses with Doric columns
and marble steps. A plaque or a stone lion
sets them apart, but all are the same,

and, the big snow over, one in whiteness.
Outside wrought-iron gates, men stroke silk top hats,
women wave puffed sleeves. Fashions later,

we hailed a horseless taxi near The Row,
restless before another wedding, ours,
at work until we had to leave, in jeans

to be slipped off, my dress slung on his arm.
In a house uptown, we'd stand in awe
and celebrate the *mystery of marriage,*

uttering *Blessed art Thou,* not in belief
but ceremony. Hadn't our bodies wed,
hadn't we whispered vows to one another,

stronger than prayers memorized and chanted?
We looked back for a sign — a tree, a sparrow,
to mark this hour. Far off, a small spark,

a match, perhaps, suddenly flamed larger,
and columns blazed. Our vows were of the present
and future, but not this past: The Row,

grand-nineties look, hints of a Greek temple,
like marriage wine, is and was, long before us.
I thought that light had gone out. I was wrong.

We pass The Row each day, and have, and will,
each of us separate, both the same,
in high sunlight or in the salmon glow

at sundown, streetlamps started, burning low.
It is always Greece, the coach-and-driver wedding,
and the cab to our own vows, all one, all now.

LATE SNOW

First day of spring and winter can't let go.
I can't let go, through dread, of silver maybes:
of black that glows, as a cowbird's sheen,
of gray dawns when, mud-colored, slow,

the river to the west gurgles hosannas.
Now near the end of the middle of my life,
all I want is more wakings like this one,
to watch day break, hear the trash truck growl,

glance at my love's body, shadowy
under bed linen, shaping a luminous question.
I'll have a pale sun strike the air conditioner,
turn its ice particles into asterisks,

and wake a bewitched maple that will bloom
despite the park's tossed soda cans, dope fumes,
dog piss, rat poison, banal conversation —
green as on the first day of Creation.

In Place of Belief

Tradition threatens. Far off, I heard bells,
those pebbly ones that top scrolls in the ark.
Up ahead, gargoyles with toothy snarls
glared from a synagogue on Central Park.

I'd read the place grew from a wooden house.
When razed, its holy innards were sent on
to other temples: lamps, goblets for wine,
pointers, and floorboards that soak up prayers.

Once, turning thirteen, called to the ark,
I touched a scroll whose black letters blurred
like scuff marks on sand the sea had washed.
I listened for God's bass and heard instead

chatter, a squeaky platform. Shuddering,
how could I even mumble sacred songs.
Only now, through doors of a massive building
whose ark is curtained shut, silver bells ring.

2

Lao Tsu told it best: The way is nameless.
The real cannot be seen. Still I make lists
of miracles, and never mind eternal.
Here, lilies unfurl in rocky soil;

a papery plant blooms into silver dollars;
grackles bob in a ring like a holy synod.
Earthly, but so was God's roll call of items
to build a chest for the Law: acacia wood,

brass rings, indigo curtains, names of things
transient but fit to hold all that endures.
Whatever comes, the voice that follows lightning
or Billie's tones, the hush after she sings;

the cloud that inks the field or my neighbor's shadow,
liquid in moonlight, I would eavesdrop, spy,
and keep watch on the chance, however slight,
that the unseen might dazzle into sight.

3

An image reveals what we're afraid we mean.
In Nadar's print, a banker's palm lies empty,
rigid as a saint's in benediction,
and coppery, as though it still holds money.

Of course. An actor tells me it is gesture,
not utterance, that contradicts a line,
the twisted silk scarf a dead giveaway,
the woman's knife marks on the table linen,

more than clipped words, disclose her wrath.
You turn from ritual, though once you stood solemn
at our unorthodox wedding, in the faith
but bare of symbols, and suddenly fished satin

from a side pocket to cover your head.
For your father, you explained. I nodded,
and said no more. Such lapses have been rare
in you, loyal to science and human care.

4

Hands are truth-tellers, sometimes informers,
and treacherous. They creep out of disguises.
The gilt hand a friend gave me in Cancun,
blessed by a priest, points to the work undone.

Rodin carved hands that beg, clench, rise in anger,
or throb in sex, revealing the invisible
bodies they serve. One pair of hands in marble
shapes a cathedral's tower, with tapered fingers

that touch as a clamshell shuts — in love, in fear.
Henri Matisse lived as an unbeliever
but for one hand that sketched hands locked in prayer.
And you, like Flaubert's Dr. Larivière,

practice virtue without believing in it.
Now you reach for a twig to stake clematis
with hands always ungloved to palpate flesh
and probe a virus strain that causes death.

5

Autumn, and Hopkins first glimpsed silver-on-silver
Northern Lights, which roused "delightful fear"
as rays pulsed like a sun bursting through clouds.
Notes wrestle in his journals; side by side

some challenge God, others caress the whorls
he called star knots in a thick, weathered aspen,
yew leaves, the horned violet, the bluebell,
the ruck and crease of waves that flash through stones.

I thought of Hopkins and his praise today
when I studied the pure symmetry
of cross-stitches on an oak leaf's underside
and knew that love is nothing less than accuracy:

the fire that I lit this morning flares
sapphire and violet as it gasps for air;
the blackening logs, the smell of cedar wood
are what I have of an evasive God.

6

To Hedda Sterne

The painter spoke at last: "My dark is luminous.
For those who see, the midday sun can blur
sharp outlines." When she wheeled her chair toward mine,
blank eyes fondled the dahlias I gave her.

Walls are stripped of canvases, the ladder gone
that she had climbed to paint angles of light,
where brushstrokes had flown in constant motion
but with no fixed point, like her faith and art.

Suddenly she waved my hand aside
and, trembling, but with startling exactness,
poured sherry for us both in crystal glasses.
"Shapes are vague now, but I have memorized

the clock, the *OED*, the china shelf."
She pointed to them — in the wrong locations.
Art does not ask fidelity to life
but ardent precision. So does belief.

5

Readers

St. Anne Teaching the Virgin to Read,
Juan de Juni, Valladolid Cathedral, Spain

It's the persimmon in St. Anne's hand
as she teaches the Virgin to read,

the parchment, grainy, cool as leaves, the binding,
the sly glance, the bodies coarse and dense,

as mother and daughter, carved in radiant wood,
search for words. Hands are not joined,

but what is that compared with eyes that burn,
red-yellow gowns that fall to the floor as one.

The child touches letters M and MA
for Mary, like the Chinese brushstroke moon,

Hebrew *mem,* Greek *mu,* the Babylonian
mas mas mas of the student who digs signs

in earth and notches clay. Shaped like a bridge,
suspended, the raised M links two cultures,

two readers. It's touch that stirs words off pages,
even for the monk who inked a Bible,

drew saints' heads in the crooks of L's,
then ran his fingers lightly down the jewels

on gold covers. And it is the hunger,
as in this Mary's eyes, to know the letters

that peer through letters, to find the writer
before the writer, and for all the mysteries

of the flesh, the fruit, the word, the story:
Persimmon. Parchment. Try it: *Mama, Mary.*

Northern Mockingbird

Day comes up like dirt islands at low tide,
revealing what I cannot lose: gulls circling,
a skiff upended, caulked for a new launching,
a tern flying in place before a dive,

lobster traps hidden in phragmites
to catch — what, Moses? Long days promise miracles.
But there, on the juniper's topmost bough,
a bird does its high-wire act, twisting

as though for ballast, singing two-note phrases:
the years, the years. Rank bird, how it persists.
Showoff. Not singing. Mimicking, cleverly
mocking my dream to hold this day forever.

The northern mockingbird, of the same species
Walt Whitman heard on this same shore, and penciled
in his diary. Not the same bird, of course,
but with a heritage, a long line,

if not long life. Its message is harsh.
I won't see it forever, nor the juniper
sprung up inside the center of a rosebush
grown, somehow undaunted, on dry sand,

unless my song can recycle this day
and pass it on like flotsam, in a sea
that inlays glass, wears white stones smooth,
and tosses them, shining, on this shore.

Come, love, let us run into the waves
past the rosebush on fire, dodging clamshells,
though an echoing bird calls, *years, the years,*
and a worn fence unrolls like thumbed pages.

Chosen

My own possessions books and one great love,
I marvel at how Leonardo's Virgin
looks up from words to hear the one Word: *chosen*.

Now here's a saltier miracle of birth:
No Gabriel, but St. John of the waters
has blessed a sign, TERNS NESTING, in streaked letters,

stuck on a sandy lane fenced with thin wire
to make a wall you feel but do not see.
Read FOOTPATH, and enter at your peril.

Not song but shrieks. Wingflaps. White birds dip fast
and wheel, a black-capped sky patrol, their eggs
the colors of rock and pied for camouflage.

The chicks hatched — odor of moss, slime, algae —
red bills struck out to sea, they drop for fish
one by one by one, sliding down air.

Don't glance at their young. And don't lose heart
or sink in quicksand while envying quick flight.
Onshore, walkers are weighty, each alone,

faint smiles, eyes low, and only footprints cross.
Random, directionless. Not so these fliers.
They're picked to breed ternness, chosen for

the hunter's scan, the dive, the climb. And I,
whose heirs are words, wish for them: fly,
terns, ride long over water and survive.

WALK!

Arise, and take up thy bed, and walk.
—— Mark 2:9

Rise up and stagger now on the sea road
at sunset, where clouds vanish like bandages

that fall from cured flesh, where lavender nods.
Wade through wild roses poking up through sand.

At low tide, a green island looms so close
that, though fumbling, you might trudge through water,

never mind leap or glide, and reach dry sand.
Once you strode high, unbending, and you fell

like a tree. When strangers helped you rise,
a smile masked rage. Science your guide, you'd been

the healer, not the healed. Days of rain
when others shot the stairs, leaped into waves,

swam inlets. Bend to the knife. And even after,
you said, no miracle. A surgeon's skill.

But here are wonders. You limp past scrub pines
and hear the salt wind play a lyre-shaped oak.

Wake to flaws; the sea tosses back shells
brightest when they are chipped, snapped, and broken.

Queen Hermione, perfect in stone,
stirs, steps off a fluted post, and stumbles,

never to soar. We slog. We tramp the road
of possibility. Give me your arm.

In the Foreground

In Monet's painting, men building a pier
stand out, their forms reflected in the water
while houses of Parliament dissolve in fog.

Workers cast images that say it twice:
No law, no sovereign power, can be as clear
as planks sanded to make a wharf, each log

raised up a ladder thin as a bracelet.
No act passes as calmly as a barge
sails under a bridge in a blue daybreak.

His Paris at war, Monet fled and stared
through a window at the Thames. In his vision,
life in the foreground outshone large decisions.

Here at the shore, a swan skimming the bay
goes double, mirrored upside down in water.
Two trees bend, like the towers built to sway,

or so I read. No facts are as clear
as lines reeling out silver from a pier,
or a surfer rising to stand in wind,

no rubble plainer than shadow-pocked sand.
The dream you wake from is another dream.
Horror to peace. A swimmer heads home,

a sailor unfolds canvas. A cormorant
spreads wings like vestments for the eucharist.
The terns fall silent now as sun-clouds darken,

and in the city, where smoke-clouds still hover,
a woman looks skyward, hoping for rain.
Up front — pier, ladder, barges — things are clear.

LESSON FROM THE COIN

You saw a penny gleam on tacky asphalt,
pried it loose, and slid it into roots
of a violet bed, one hand raised in blessing.
Remember the rose and the god, the coin

you gave me, struck with a full-blown rose?
On the flip side is Helios, sun god,
his thick hair so disheveled it might rise
out of the tiny frame. The rose of Rhodes —

each petal flares and tapers to furl inward —
would check the god's unruly flight and fall,
and, sure as sunrise, lift him from the sea.
Two sides — wildness and order — pull as one.

My coin's a copy of a silver drachma,
fourth century B.C.E., dropped on Greek sand.
Perhaps the loser was a Hebrew scribe
who copied history, a merchant sailor,

or a Greek writer before his exile,
and the finder was a Roman soldier.
I hold the hands that held its ancestor
traded or given, tossed, earned, hoarded, loaned,

not of one purse or pocket, never owned,
a wanderer, a new minting, a sign.
Hand touches hand, connected by a coin,
a wedge, a corner, a wish for the world.

Loss

Look back through the cedars
to where the rhododendron
shed blooms and gained dry hooks.
Observe the deadly nightshade

and vines that strangle lindens,
climbers with hooks and thorns.
Recall the afternoon
when we missed God's voice

walking in the garden
in the cool of day,
when, laughing, you declared
that voice could never walk.

It bellowed out our sins,
such as blank inattention
that made us turn away
with a helpless shrug

from sorrow at the gate;
the worst, indifference
to the cardinal's warning,
to whale talk, raven call

in languages not our own.
While gazing at each other,
we missed the lightning flash
that forced a tree to bear

one peach in a false spring.
The bearded phragmites
bowed gravely, like priests,
seen but never known

in the minute particulars
that give a name to praise.
The news announcements came.
A squadron of geese called

and drowned the leaves' percussion.
A gale eroded dunes,
and like Masaccio's pair,
his hands blocking his eyes,

hers covering her sex,
we left for a bare land.
Our loss was of each thing
that had been lost on us:

the aphid on the rose,
elm blight, a stranger's grief.
Now observe dry soil
until it blesses you.

Hear the long vibrato
of sacred rage, and listen
for cries in a treeless country,
unshaded from the light.

CIMICIFUGA

White pipe cleaners,
chalky flags in wind,
sprang up unplanted
at the wood's edge,
near rocks and icy moss,
in late November,
whose days thirst for light.
What an unpromising start,
conceived last summer
in the droppings of a bird
that fueled at my feeder
for the long flight.
Even its English names —
black cohosh,
snakeroot —
sound as though someone
didn't want it.

Is this what death is like,
hope before darkness,
or is it waking?
On this land once,
a dying woman
of the Montauk people
ground star-white flowers
into a paste mixed with snow
and drank to her recovery.
Cimicifuga racemosa,
windsocks riding air
after roses are ash,

your name a rainbow of vowels
that sing of light,
glimmer in bone-dry woods,
blaze in our winter night,
deliver us.

Harp Song

Near the shore, this white oak split in two
struggles to endure sea winds and grow,
twin columns chapped and branches stripped of leaves.

The bark is grooved like an islander's face
as he sails out for bass with pots and trawl,
and in the worst storms sings in a raspy,

whiskey voice haul-aways learned from whalers.
While gale-force winds snapped the unbending hickory,
lashed a cedar, and ripped out an elm

in acid soil worn smooth and unsustaining
even of grass, the doubled oak goes on.
Both arms reach skyward. The trunk is bent

into a U, the shape of a harp, unstrung.
In gales, it slides from one note to another,
portamento, like a soprano's glide.

I breathe deep when I pass: a song of rage
rises from wood that has been salt-bleached, cut,
whipped to buckle, and has, instead, stood fast.

Tempests roll out chords, pick the harp-tree clean
with pizzicati, and weave eerie arpeggios.
I have heard wooden harps whose strings fell slack

for centuries — one cast down when Deor,
once a king's prized singer of battle songs,
found a new harpist in his chair at court,

his own name lost, and moaned: *it, too, may pass;*
but this harp cries out *survive* in anger,
stringless, played by winds, to a silent god.

WAVES

The lilt and rock, the wheel of spray, the burst,
the flash of waves that explode in a hard rain.

Perhaps they are the dead, their watermark
the signatures of shipwrecked passengers,

or coded messages from men and women
desperate to tell what they have seen.

Speed, thunder, surprise. The jarring thump
of low bass drums, the dancer's leap and bow,

the gospel singer's growl, the pause, the shout,
dodging the beat, notes jammed with syllables,

the hums, mumbles, and cries, the choruses,
cymbals that gleam in sudden white-gold light.

Breakers roared when Caedmon sang Creation
in verse with the rhythmic pull of oars.

Rollers boom on a shore I cannot see
and tie me to flood-dead, quake-dead, war-dead,

disaster-dead, or dead ripped from the stars.
As I trudge in the shallows, sliding in wrack,

order snapped apart like a broken string,
each end still aloft, trembling in air,

the sea ahead, the roadways drowned behind,
a wave shimmers, taking its time to fall.

How all that matters is to stand fast
on the ridge that's left, and hear the music.

NOTES

"The Broken String." Itzhak Perlman's performance of Mendelssohn's Violin Concerto took place at Avery Fisher Hall in New York on November 18, 1995. The story of the broken string was reported in the *Houston Chronicle,* February 10, 2001.

"Blue in Green." Miles Davis, trumpet; John Coltrane, tenor. I first heard *Kind of Blue* on a Columbia CD.

"Kol Nidrei, September 2001." The attack on September 11 preceded by only sixteen days the chanting of Kol Nidrei ("All Vows") on Yom Kippur, a high holiday in Judaism. Its ritual enacts a legal plea to cancel all promises made in the preceding year and in the year to come.

"Orson's Shadow." The title is borrowed from a play by Austin Pendleton. Orson Welles, the great actor and director, died in 1985. This poem is set in the 1970s, by which time he suffered a decline in his career.

"Art Tatum at the Gee-Haw Stables." I'm grateful for *Too Marvelous for Words: The Life and Genius of Art Tatum,* by James Lester.

"Origins." The stanza in italics contains phrases culled from *Mourt's Relation: A Journal of the Pilgrims at Plymouth,* edited by Dwight B. Heath. The journal is thought to have been written by Edward Winslow and William Bradford and was originally published by George Morton. I first read the passage quoted by Thoreau in his *Cape Cod.*

"Collectors." Photographs of Neruda's house and its destruction are in *Pablo Neruda: Absence and Presence,* by Luis Poirot, with translations of the text by Alastair Reid.

"The Horror." For details of Chaim Soutine's life I am indebted to *Soutine,* by Monroe Wheeler (Museum of Modern Art, 1950) and "Abstracting Soutine," by Arthur C. Danto (*The Nation,* August 24/31, 1998).

"Death." Second-line beat. In a traditional New Orleans jazz funeral, the band swings into improvisational jazz, but only after they have played Christian hymns from church to cemetery. Leaving the burial, at a respectful distance, the lead trumpeter sounds a two-note riff and the drummers roll out the second-line. In *Rejoice When You Die: The New Orleans Jazz Funerals,* by Vernal Bagneris, photographs by Leo Touchet. Also, Louis Armstrong talks of the second-line in an Edward R. Murrow documentary, *Satchmo the Great.*

Passages in italics are my translations of *Beowulf,* lines 3164 and 3145.

"St. Sulpice." Jacob and the angel, Genesis 32:25–33.

"The Crow Man." "Every angel terrifies" is from Rilke's *Duino Elegies.* "*Seven palaces*" refers to the Merkabah mystic's journey in a storm through seven heavens, with seven palaces and seven doors. In *Major Trends in Jewish Mysticism,* by Gershom Scholem. Also, Harold Bloom writes of the angel Metatron, and his journey through the heavens, in *Omens of Millennium: The Gnosis of Angels, Dreams, and Resurrection.*

"The Row." "Each of us separate, both the same," varied in this poem, is from the wedding service in Judaism.

"In Place of Belief." *You practice virtue without believing in it.* Said, in the third person, of Dr. Larivière, who appears briefly, nobly, in Flaubert's *Madame Bovary.*

"Harp Song." Deor: a deposed court harpist in an Anglo-Saxon poem of that title. The poem's refrain is *Thaes ofereode, thisses swa maeg,* or *That is over; this will be, too.*

"Waves." For the phrase "thump / of low bass drums," I am indebted to Walt Whitman's *Specimen Days.*